SE⌔
TI

*Exploring a
Coral Reef*

by Michael Sandler

Harcourt
SCHOOL PUBLISHERS

Cover (tl), ©Charles Palek/Animals Animals, (tc) ©Mitsuaki Iwago/Minden Pictures, (tr) ©Konrad Wothe/Minden Pictures, Inc., (cl) ©Gary Griffen/Animals Animals, (c) ©Franz Lanting/Minden Pictures, (cr) Vix Cox/Peter Arnold, Inc.; p.3, ©Charles Palek/Animals Animals; p.4, ©Gary Griffen/Animals Animals; p.5, ©Robert Maier/Animals Animals; p.6, ©Mitsuaki Iwago/Minden Pictures; p.7, ©Linda Richardson/Peter Arnold, Inc.; p.8–9, ©Vic Cox/Peter Arnold, Inc.; p.10, ©Franz Lanting/Minden Pictures; p.11, ©Bruno P. Zehnder/Peter Arnold, Inc.; p.12, ©Tom Vezo/Peter Arnold, Inc.; p.13–14, ©Charles Palek/Animals Animals.

Printed in Mexico

ISBN 10: 0-15-351031-5
ISBN 13: 978-0-15-351031-1

Ordering Options
ISBN 10: 0-15-350602-4 (Grade 5 On-Level Collection)
ISBN 13: 978-0-15-350602-4 (Grade 5 On-Level Collection)
ISBN 10: 0-15-357956-0 (package of 5)
ISBN 13: 978-0-15-357956-1 (package of 5)

"It's incredible," Hawk told me. "There are so many fish. It's like swimming inside an aquarium. Also, the coral are unbelievable. They're red, blue, and purple! Imagine an explosion of fireworks!"

I had known Hawk for over twenty years, yet every time he talked about coral reefs, I was blown away by his excitement. Some of the best, he said, were the reefs of the Philippines. This country is made up of thousands of islands in the South Pacific Ocean. There are more than seven thousand islands in all. The waters around these islands are filled with coral. Some of the world's richest sea life can be found in the Philippines.

Hawk had been to the Philippines many times. He was a very skilled scuba diver. He loved to explore the country's waters. Hawk called it the ultimate diving spot. I was excited by what he told me. I made up my mind. I was going to see it for myself.

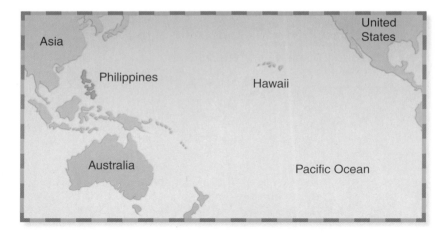

Coral Reefs

Coral reefs are found only in warm, shallow waters. These reefs are made up of groups of tiny animals called coral. When coral die, they leave behind hard skeletons. The skeletons build up and form reefs. New coral grow on top. The reefs grow bigger and bigger.

The coral can be hard or soft. They come in many colors. They come in different shapes. Some look like streamers. Others are shaped like horns. Some look almost like brains.

Not only coral live here. Plants grow on the reefs. Animals come here for food. Over a hundred thousand kinds of animals have been counted. More sea animals are found around coral reefs than any other place in the ocean.

There are sea worms and shrimp. There are lobsters and crabs. There are snails, clams, and mussels. Starfish and sponges fix onto the coral. Thousands of kinds of fish swim by.

Getting to the Philippines wasn't easy. The journey was long. It took nearly fifteen hours. I took one suitcase filled with gear. Hawk had told me what to bring.

I had fins. I had a mask and snorkel. I even had an underwater camera. I was ready to dive into the water.

My first stop was Manila. This is the capital city of the Philippines. Then I had to switch planes. The second plane was tiny. It had just eight seats. The internal area of the plane was no bigger than a minivan. It felt like a car with wings!

The tiny plane started moving. I felt a little nervous. Could it really fly? Fly it did! In just about an hour, the trip was over. I was in Palawan. This was my final destination. It is known as one of the best places in the country to see coral.

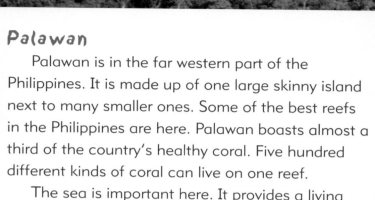

Palawan

Palawan is in the far western part of the Philippines. It is made up of one large skinny island next to many smaller ones. Some of the best reefs in the Philippines are here. Palawan boasts almost a third of the country's healthy coral. Five hundred different kinds of coral can live on one reef.

The sea is important here. It provides a living to many residents. Many are fishers. Others work in the tourist industry. They run hotels. They run restaurants. They run dive shops. Meanwhile, tourists come from all over the world. Many come just to dive.

Wow! This place sure was different. Back in New York, it was freezing. The city had just been hit by a blizzard. The streets were covered with snow.

Here in Palawan it was just the opposite. There wasn't any snow. The island was steaming hot. It was lush. It was green. I had to adjust. This was quite a change.

The ocean was amazing. It was a shiny flat pan of blue-green water. White rock islands stuck out of the sea. Around them were the reefs. How was I going to get to them? I would take a boat, of course!

Bancas

The banca boat is very common in the Philippines. It is used for fishing. It ferries people from island to island. It is even used to deliver mail!

What do banca boats look like? Some are big. They can be large enough for thirty or forty passengers. Others are small. Many are just big enough for a single fisher. The boats are made out of wood. Two bamboo runners keep them stable. A banca boat rarely sinks. It can stand up to heavy seas.

The next morning, I woke up early. I was ready to head out. The beautiful ocean was waiting for me.

I had hired a banca and crew. The captain was named Carlo. With him were two assistants. We would spend a week on the boat. We would move from one spot to another, exploring the sea.

During the day, we would snorkel. At night, we would sleep on the boat. For seven days, it would be my home. The boat skimmed across the water. I looked down at the reef. It lay just below the water's surface. The colors of the coral showed through the clear water. Suddenly, Carlo shut off the motor.

"Here," he said, "we will start."

I dove into the water. Through my mask, everything was crystal clear. Hawk was right! It was like swimming inside an aquarium. This was really incredible! The reef was just an arm's length beneath me. I stared at large, hard coral covered with a group of purple starfish.

Nearby, soft pink coral waved and fluttered like leaves in a breeze. Between their fronds, pesky little fish were dancing. I gently touched an anemone with the toe of my flipper. As I did, tiny tentacles recoiled. Then, through the corner of my mask, I saw Carlo wave. I turned in his direction. To my right, I saw that he was pointing to a giant clam—it was opening its massive mouth!

Over the next six days, I took in one incredible dive after another. I saw more fish than I could remember. I saw pipefish. I saw manta rays and sea cucumbers. I watched spiny lobsters crawl. I even saw a few sharks!

Meanwhile, the coral were amazing! There were white-pink coral gardens. There were coral fields filled with hundreds of sea fans.

After each dive, Carlo gave me an explanation. He told me the names of every creature we had seen. Then he would answer any questions that I had.

"Do many people come here to see the coral?" I asked Carlo.

"More and more each year," he said. "On the one hand, it's great business. On the other, it's a problem. Some throw garbage into the water. More people means more litter and debris. Careless divers can hurt the reef. They want to take specimens home. I always warn them: look, don't touch."

Suddenly, I felt embarrassed. I remembered the anemone I'd touched. I wouldn't do that again!

Carlo went on. "Boats can be a problem, too. Dropped anchors can smash coral. We've got to be careful with the reef. If it dies, there will be nothing for people to see."

The Changing Reef

Palawan's reefs took centuries to grow. Sadly, however, they can be destroyed much more quickly. Some threats are natural. Storms bring giant waves. These waves can smash coral to bits. Heavy rains can wash soil off the land. The soil ends up in the water, and it blocks out the sunlight that coral need to grow.

Other threats, such as careless diving, come from humans. Destructive fishing is another example. Reef fish are highly sought by restaurants. To catch them alive—so that they stay fresh longer—some fishers use a poison called cyanide. They squirt the poison into the water, and it stuns the fish but does not kill them. However, the poison can kill the coral and other reef dwellers as well.

Authorities are working to stop this kind of fishing. They teach fishers about the harm it causes. "Fish need the reef," they explain. "If you kill the reef, the fish will disappear. You are killing your own future."

Another threat to reefs is harder to control. This is changing water temperatures. Water that's too warm causes coral to get "bleached" and lose their color. Then they die. Some scientists think that global warming may be causing ocean waters to warm up. If this continues, reefs around the world will die.

When my trip was over, I hopped off the boat. Afterward, I thanked Carlo and headed for the airport. The trip had been incredible. I had learned a lot about the reef, its residents, and the threats that reefs were facing.

I couldn't wait to get home to tell Hawk everything! It felt like I had done more than just visit a new country. It felt like I had visited another world—the underwater world of the coral reef.

As my plane took off, I stared out through the window. I looked down at the shimmering water below. I didn't know when I was coming back, but I was sure of one thing. My first visit to a coral reef wouldn't be my last!

Think Critically

1. Why is the narrator's friend, Hawk, important to the events of the book?

2. Compare and contrast Palawan to your own town.

3. What kind of person is Carlo?

4. Coral grow slowly but can change very quickly. What can cause changes to a reef?

5. Would you like to take a dive trip to a coral reef? Why or why not?

 Science

Danger Diagram Draw a diagram to illustrate the dangers that coral reefs are facing. Then write a paragraph to explain your diagram.

 School-Home Connection Share what you learned about coral reefs with a friend or family member. Discuss why it's important to try to save coral reefs.